Wash Up!

Gwenyth Swain

First Avenue Editions/Minneapolis

small world

To find out more about the pictures in this book, turn to page 22.
To find out more about sharing this book with children, turn to page 24.

The photographs in this book are reproduced with the permission of: © Sylvie Villeger/Photo Researchers, Inc., front cover; © Trip/J. Wakelin, back cover, 16; ©Trip/J. King, p. 1; © Trip/Eric Smith, p. 3; © Michael S. Yamashita/CORBIS, p. 4; © Wolfgang Kaehler, p. 5; © Trip/S. Grant, p. 6; © Paul J. Buklarewicz, p. 7; © Elaine Little/World Photo Images, p. 8, 13; © Trip/D. Clegg, p. 9; © Margaret Miller/Photo Researchers, Inc., p. 10; © Trip/H. Rogers, p. 11; © Dean Conger/CORBIS, p. 12; © Fotografia, Inc./CORBIS, p. 14; © Nancy Durell-McKenna/Panos Pictures, p. 15; © Jeanie Woodcock, Reflections Photolibrary/CORBIS, p. 17; © Lawrence Migdale/Photo Researchers, Inc., p. 18; © Trip/David Pluth, p. 19; © Margie Politzer/Photo Researchers, Inc., p. 20; © Trip/J. Dennis, p. 21.

First Avenue Editions
An imprint of Lerner Publishing Group
241 First Avenue North
Minneapolis, MN 55401 U.S.A.

Website address: www.lernerbooks.com

Library of Congress Cataloging-in-Publication Data

Swain, Gwenyth, 1961–
    Wash Up! / by Gwenyth Swain.
      p.   cm. — (Small world)
    ISBN: 1–57505–161–3 (pbk. : alk. paper)
      1. Hygiene—Juvenile literature. [1. Cleanliness.] I. Title.
    II. Small world (Minneapolis, Minn.)
    RA777.S93 2002
    613'.4—dc21   2001000050

Manufactured in the United States of America
1 2 3 4 5 6 – JR – 07 06 05 04 03 02

Are there days when you
need a good cleaning?

Did you decide to
slide in something icky?

Did your favorite food
leave you all sticky?

When you need a good washing,
there's no time to waste.

Take a break and jump in a lake.

Turn on the tap. Fill a pail.

Wash yourself at the nearest well.

Lather up till bubbles fly.

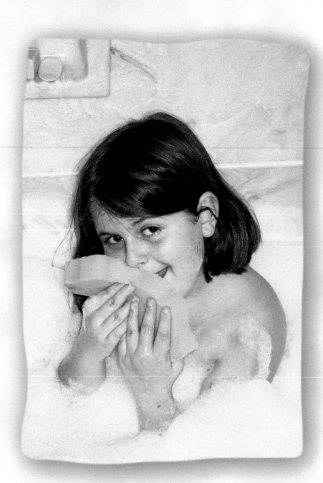

Keep the soap out of your eyes!

Scrub yourself from top to toe.

Be sure to rinse before you go.

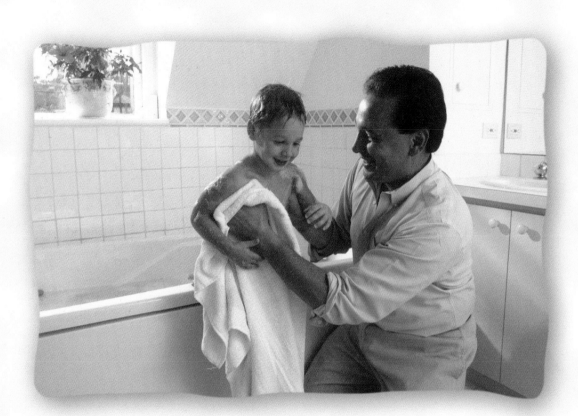

Rub down wet skin.

Flash a clean grin.

Part your hair in one neat line.

Comb it. Brush it. Make it shine.

Learn to wash yourself well,

and you can wash others, too.

Some critters need help

doing what you can do.

More about the Pictures

Front cover: A four-year-old girl has fun washing her hair.

Back cover: In Queensland, Australia, Aborigine children bathe in a *billabong,* or streambed.

Page 1: An English boy proudly shows off clean teeth.

Page 3: On a hot day in England, a baby takes a bath in a wheelbarrow.

Page 4: A group of Thai children have fun playing in the mud along the Mekong River bank.

Page 5: This boy in Bergen, Norway, discovers that it's hard to eat ice cream without getting *very* sticky.

Page 6: A boy in Long Beach, California, takes the time to wash his hands, sudsing well with soap.

Page 7: A natural hot spring on the island of Okinawa in Japan makes the perfect outdoor tub.

Page 8: At a shelter for the homeless in Manila in the Philippines, two boys rinse off after a bath.

Page 9: A large well in Lombok, Indonesia, is just the spot for a quick cleanup.

Page 10: A boy in India lathers his hair with shampoo.

Page 11: Soap bubbles make cleaning up fun for this English girl.

Page 12: Boys wash in a communal shower on the island of Java in Indonesia.

Page 13: A mother pours water from a bucket to rinse off her child in the Philippines.

Page 14: A father helps his child towel off after a bath.

Page 15: Brothers in Calcutta, India, brush their teeth using their fingers and fine ash.

Page 16: On the island of Sumatra, in Indonesia, a mother combs out snarls in her daughter's hair.

Page 17: This girl in England has a lot of hair to brush!

Page 18: A girl in Albany, California, wipes her face while looking in the bathroom mirror.

Page 19: An older sister washes the baby of the family in a big round bowl in Kampala, Uganda.

Page 20: A *mahout*—someone who keeps elephants and trains them to work—helps one of his animals get clean in a river in Thailand. Do you help your pets stay clean?

Page 21: Children bathe on a beach in Indonesia.

A Note to Adults on Sharing This Book

Help your child become a lifelong reader. Read this book together, taking turns as you both read out loud. Look over the photographs and choose your favorites. Sound out new words and go back to them later for review. Then try these "extensions"—activities that extend the experience of reading and build discussion and problem-solving skills.

Talk about Washing Up

All around the world, people wash themselves in different ways. Discuss with your child the reasons why people wash themselves. Take a closer look at the pictures in this book. In how many different locations and in how many kinds of containers are children shown bathing themselves? How do the ways of bathing differ from your child's usual bath? How are they the same?

Wall of Washing

With your child, gather pictures of people and animals washing up. Look through magazines for pictures of people brushing their teeth or animals grooming themselves. Search the newspapers for advertisements for your favorite soap and shampoo—or for your dog's flea bath. Take a camera to the zoo and snap shots of animals cleaning themselves or soaking in pools. Then put all of these pictures on a poster board or on the wall in your bathroom. Ask your child to compare and contrast the ways that animals and people wash up.